Your Nose to Your Toes

Story by Tanya & Mairin
Illustrated by A. Simioni

Dedicated to all the caregivers doing their best
every day to foster loving and healthy relationships
with the little ones of the world.
Especially our parents, the best of the best.

Your toes or your nose
Your toes or your nose
Baby always chooses
Which way this massage goes

I warm up my hands
And ask your permission
My pressure is gentle
And for you I am just smitten

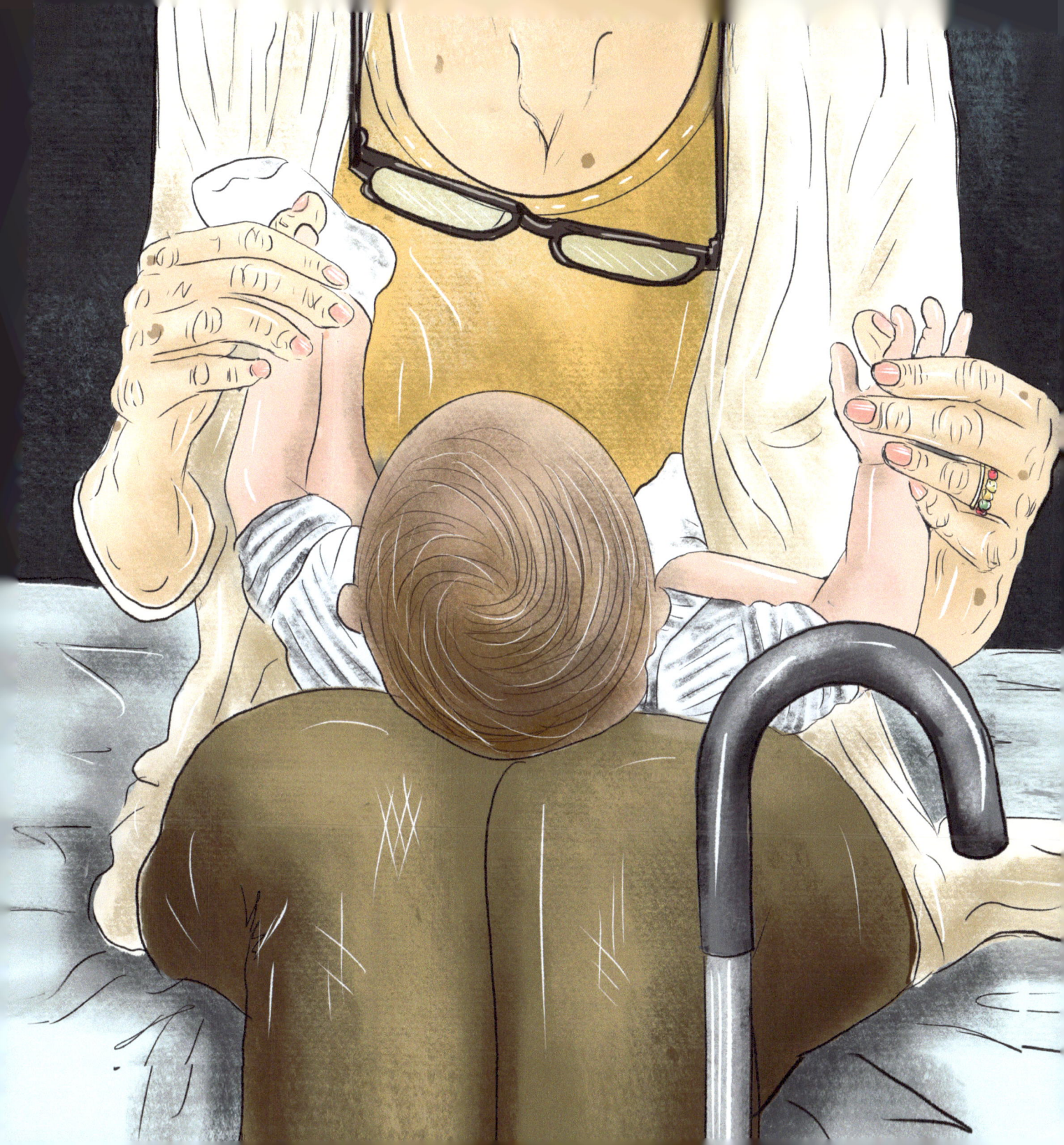

My hands hug your legs
So squishy and sweet
I glide my hands down
From your hip to your feet

I start with one leg
But won't forget the other
This time is so special
And I love being together

I gently massage
Each little piggy
Giving a little more pressure
So that you don't feel wiggly

Some babies are more ticklish
And that is okay
Your perfect uniqueness
In my head will stay

I softly sweep across your chest
Like I am opening a book
Staring into each other's eyes
With your sweet baby looks

The sun and the moon
Shine brightly onto you
Gentle finger walks along your tummy
Spelling I Love You

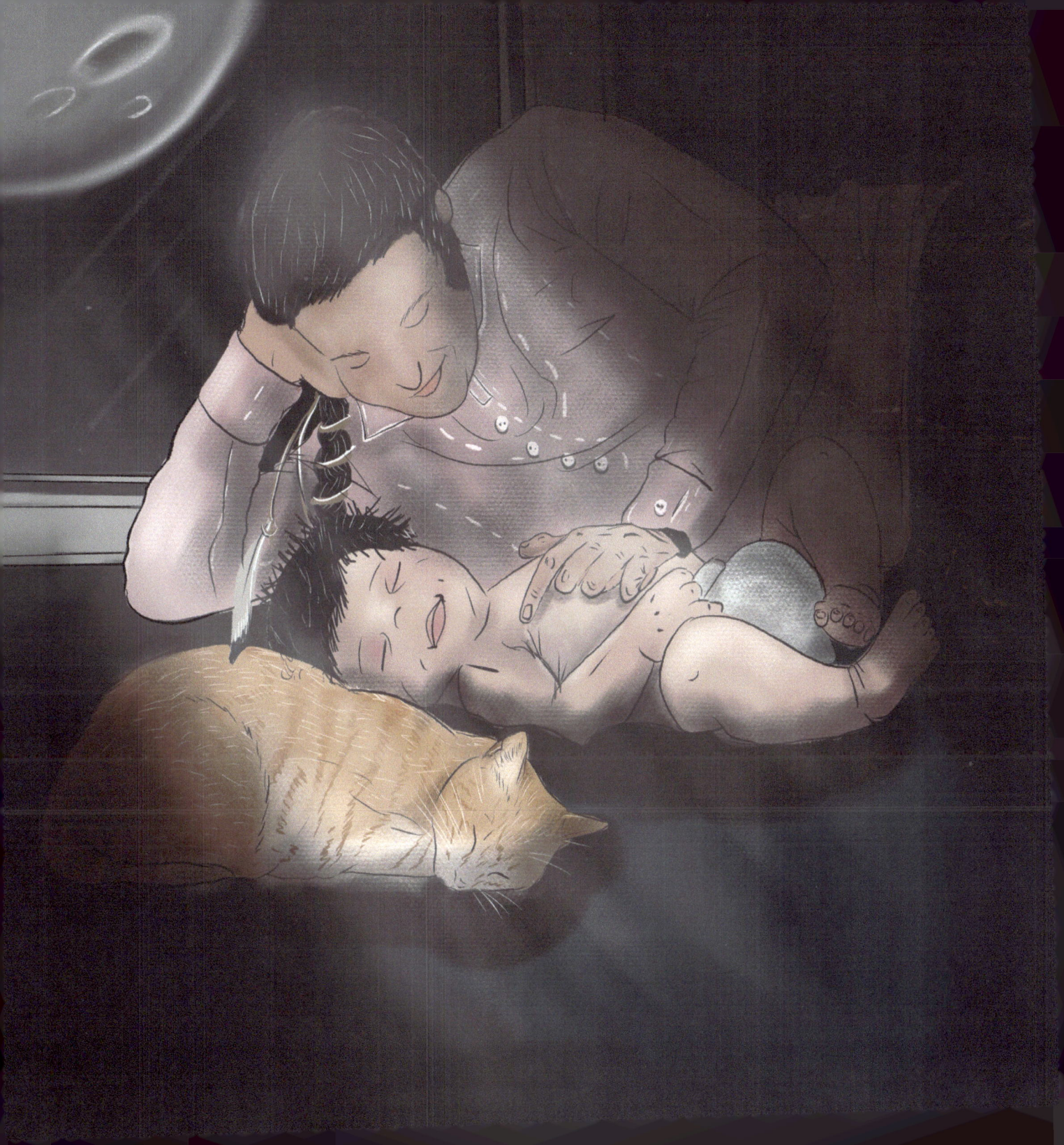

Wringing chubby little arms
Soft from your shoulders to your wrist
Draining the tension away
For us, sweet baby, only love exists

Your hands I gently massage
I want to hold them forever
You'll use them to reach and explore
But for now, let's just be together

You've been lying on your back
I know it's been a little while
But before tummy time
I trace your eyes, nose, and smile

I sweep my fingertips along your face
From the center to the sides
Across eyebrows, cheekbones,
and your jaw line
With soft, circular glides

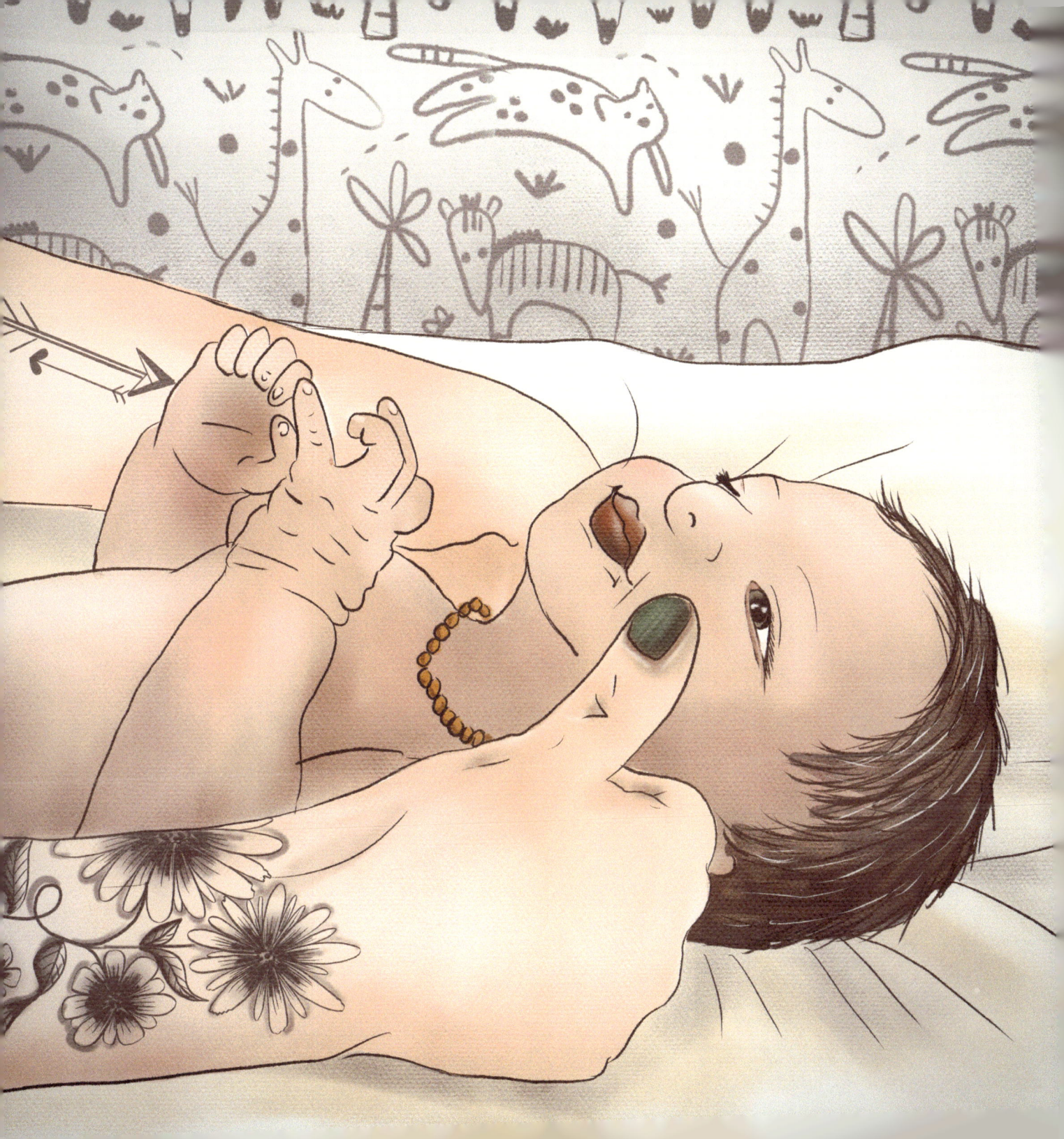

Are you ready for tummy time?
If yes, let's gently roll over
I can lay you on my lap
So we can be closer

I comb down your back
Where your hair might grow long
Downward strokes to your feet
You're getting so strong!

Now that this massage is nearly over
Our hearts are aligned
Same time, same place tomorrow?
Sweet baby of mine.

The End.

Together, Tanya and Mairin are great friends who also happen to co-own Pomegranate Grove Massage & Wellness Centre, a busy clinic in southern Ontario where they practice as massage therapists. Their mission is to create an inclusive and caring environment where everyone feels welcome, with the dream of continuing to support their wonderful community through health care and charitable efforts. They are proud to donate 10% of proceeds from *Your Nose to Your Toes* to their local Children's Foundation.

More information on this worthy organization
can be found at childrensfoundation.org

TANYA AZZOPARDI is a Registered Massage Therapist who is passionate about health care, fitness and incorporating her science background into treatments with clients. Tanya is extremely giving and engaged in her community, running many events for local charities and organizations. She enjoys spending time with her many friends and family, especially her husband, Jon, and two children, Ben and Lylah.

MAIRIN C DA MAREN is a Registered Massage Therapist and yoga teacher who loves working with pregnant and postpartum women in her practice. Mairin can often be found at home with her dogs and family or spending time outdoors. She lives with her husband and two children, Cora and Francesca.